Love Pain

Love is painful, but the pain is
certainly a blessing

By

Raymond Becky

Table of contents

Chapter 1
Chapter 2
Chapter 3
Chapter 4
Chapter 5
Chapter 6
Chapter 7
Chapter 8
Chapter 9
Conclusion

Introductions

Love is painful because love brings growth. Love demands, transforms and is painful because love gives you a new birth.
Love brings your heart into relationship -- and when the heart is in relationship there is always pain. If you avoid the pain, you will miss all pleasures of life. With love you become human; you stand erect on earth. With love you are vertical.

Chapter 1

With love are problems. But with problems is growth -- the greater the problem, the greater the opportunity. More and more pain, too.

That's why many people never love -- it is so painful. They never become vertical.

Love never shatters you completely. It simply shatters you a little, a little bit. It shatters the crust of your ego, but the centre of the ego remains intact. Then there is a deeper pain, deeper than love, and that is of prayer -- it shatters you utterly. It is death. When you have learnt how to love, and you have learnt that the pain that love brings is a blessing in disguise, it is beautiful, then you become able and you take another step -- that step is prayer.

All lovers feel a little miserable. They would like to disappear completely, but it is not possible in human relationships. Human relationship is limited. But one learns from it, that there is a possibility: if it can happen so much in a human relationship, how much more can happen in a relationship with the Divine?

Love makes you ready to take the final jump, the quantum leap. That's what I call prayer, or you can call it meditation. You have to disappear for existence to be. Love is a training ground, a school, to learn first lessons -- of the beauty, of the blessing and benediction of disappearance; to learn that pain is blessed.

So when you are in love, or when love arises, cooperate with it, don't try resisting. People come to a compromise. The basic problem that I have been looking at is that lovers by and by come to a compromise. The compromise is: You don't hurt me, I will not hurt you. That's what marriage is. Then people become settled. They become so afraid of pain that they say, "Don't hurt me and I will not hurt you." But then when pain disappears, love also disappears. They exist together.

When you are in love, love hurts. It hurts terribly. But never resist, never create any barrier for pain. Allow it. And by and by you will see that it was a wrong interpretation. It is not really pain. It is just that something is going so deep in you that you interpret it like a pain. You don't know anything else. You are only aware of pain in your past life, in your past experience. Whenever something penetrates deep, you interpret it as pain.

Don't use the word 'pain'. When love and love's arrow goes deep into your heart, close your eyes and don't use words -- just see what it is, and you will never see it is pain. You will see it is a benediction. You will be tremendously moved by it. You will feel joyous.

Chapter 2

True Love doesn't bring Sadness, Disappointment, Pain or Problems
Love isn't supposed to hurt. If it does, then it is absolutely not a true love.

You have probably heard a lot of people say that "love hurts" — and we all tend to follow the crowd and believe that "love hurts" but this isn't true.

Love doesn't hurt you. A person that doesn't know how to love hurts you. Don't get it twisted.

I think Love is the most incredible thing in the world — but when people lie, cheat, and betray our trust, we become bitter, we blame love — we start losing hope in love.

The worst part about the heartbreak is that we lose ourselves trying to hold on to that person who doesn't care at all.

We start saying "I am afraid to fall in love because I don't want to get hurt again"

Love isn't supposed to hurt. If it does, then it is absolutely not a true love.

Everyone says love hurts, but that is not true.
Loneliness hurts. Rejection hurts. Losing someone
hurts. Envy hurts. Everyone gets these things
confused with love, but in reality, love is the only
thing in this world that covers up all pain and makes
someone feel wonderful again. Love is the only
thing in this world that does not hurt.

I know how it feels to be broken. Been there and
experienced that kind of pain. I've been in a
relationship for 4 years but found out I've been
cheated on this whole time. When you find yourself
in a similar situation, how do you begin to trust
someone new?

It does take a lot of courage for a person to open
their heart to someone new because we all have
that fear inside of us due to bad past experience.
But don't let your past be an issue in your present
and future.

Love truly, be fearless — accept the person the
way they are — because true love sees beyond all
imperfections.

Someone who truly loves you sees what a mess
you can be, how moody you can get, and how hard
you can be to handle but still wants you.

True love makes you happy in a way that you have
never been happy before. It heals your broken
parts and lifts you up.

Don't let things and circumstances change you into
someone you're not.

If you can love the wrong person that much,
imagine how much you can love the right one
If you are in a relationship and your significant other
constantly judges you, brings out your
imperfections. Makes you feel like you are a
burden. Doesn't appreciate you and the efforts you
make for them, get out of the relationship.

Some people try to fantasize abusive relationship
— which is wrong on so many levels. As soon as
you see that you're not getting the love, attention or
respect, walk away.

Don't stress over someone who doesn't value your
worth.

Don't give up on something you really want
Your relationship should erase your tears, not your
smile. True love doesn't hurt, it heals. It brings
happiness to your life. It empowers you to become
the best version of yourself.

A real love is supposed to feel euphoric and
spontaneous.

Chapter 3

The most amazing and romantic things aren't in materialistic stuff. The things that matter the most are those little things you do every day to show significant other that you care and that you're thinking of them. When you love someone unconditionally, you'd go out of your way to make them happy and feel special.

True love knows someone's weakness and doesn't take advantage of them. It knows their flaws and still accepts them

Always remember that when love is real, it doesn't lie, cheat, pretend, hurt you or make you feel unwanted. It's supposed to be a cure to all your worries. Real love means to stay together and never give up.

You don't give up on the people you love

A person that really loves you wouldn't give up on you no matter how hard the situation is — when it's real you can't walk away.

Love, respect, and acceptance are very important in any healthy relationship.

Don't change yourself just to make someone love you. Be yourself and let the right one fall for you. People nowadays try to change you into their own definition of perfection. They get caught up in so-called "types" that makes me sick.

It's ridiculous how much society says things like "I want a girl or boy covered in tattoos, I want a boy who has a beard and lots of piercings and long hair" blah blah blah

What most of those people fail to realize is that looks change, and fade. How about a guy or woman who treats you right, who looks in your eyes and you can see how much they truly love you and admire your company?

Maybe someone who even in their worst moods will still do what they can to make you smile? That's something you should be looking for.

I believe, one day you do find someone who can turn your world around. You tell them things that you've never shared with another person. That's the person worth keeping in your life.

There are some words that we never forget, even years after a romantic relationship has ended. We all want to love and want to be loved. Sometimes, however, love stories do not end well because of

betrayal, boredom or indifference, often leading to
divorce.

When we enter into a love relationship, we want it
to last forever – at least if we are sincere about the
person and have the longing to be with them for a
lifetime. I do not think that this is an outdated
concept or that it should be. Love needs to be
foolish; love needs to be idealistic; love needs to be
adventurous in order to be true. But when we love,
we also want to feel safe, secure and protected –
surrounded by love of that partner and shielded
against the hostile outside world.

Some people claim that romantic love which lasts
for a lifetime is an illusion. I believe it is difficult to
achieve, but not impossible. Maybe, I am a
hopeless romantic, maybe naïve, maybe a fool –
but so far nothing has destroyed my utter
conviction. Although my beliefs about love have
been tested more than once, I still have faith in
love. Somewhere out there, there is a happy couple
or two who were able to maintain that undying love
for a lifetime – beyond physical or religious borders,
factors of race, age and social status. Maybe only
very few of us will be able to experience such a
bond but that is entirely irrelevant. The fact that
some people are able to live that kind of love, is
proof to me that love is not dead and that it can
last.

Chapter 4

Love and pain, they are so close together. Something that feels like the strongest love one moment, can crumble the next and vanish into thin air. What then remains is pain – the pain of a lost love, the pain of the absence of love in our lives that is often intertwined with the feeling of loneliness. In order for the pain to vanish, we have to go through different stages.

Most of us feel anger or resentment to the person who we once loved. Some of us even feel hatred. I believe that we have to walk through that pain, otherwise we may lose ourselves. Even if a love relationship does not end but becomes unhealthy, we can experience pain because we are feeling hurt – either by carelessness, the lack of loving gestures and words, or by actions that hurt us emotionally, mentally or even physically.

We all have loved and walked through the pain after that love ended. Sometimes we grow after a painful ending, sometimes we do not and only feel depressed. When processing the end of a romantic relationship, I believe that it is important to acknowledge the pain. We need to accept the lack of love in our lives and should exercise self-care and self-love. We should also understand that we cannot change the people we are with. We always want to change them but it is impossible in my view. A partner, who is pragmatic and hardly romantic, will not change overnight and probably never will.

Love should be an equal give and take. Words of affirmation should be reciprocal as they make love special. There are beautiful words that can be very unique for those two lovers. A friend of mine calls her husband of many years 'creature'. At first, I was surprised, but she says those words to him in such a loving and kind way that I could simply feel the love between those two humans.

Chapter 5

Love is complicated, love is joyful, love is painful, love is inexplicable but love should always feel unique. No one who says 'I love you' wants to hear utter silence or a careless reply. Meaningless words are either fast forgotten or even cause pain. Only words that come from the heart and soul, will stick for a lifetime in our minds as a token of that love. So I want to close this article with a little poem and the simple thought: love today with an intensity as if it was your last day.

Accept the whole. To love someone is to accept them fully for who they are, imperfections and all. Love does not seek to change. Love does not seek anything, actually. It's selfless. Love celebrates the other person for who they are as a whole. Its job is not to judge; it's to be a safe, warm and welcoming place (open arms, if you will) for the other person.If you are trying to change someone, or looking for ways to manipulate someone to get what you want, chances are that it's not really love that you're expressing or using to make decisions. Try to peel back the layers three times to figure out what's really going on. Ask yourself, why do I want to change this person? Then, ask yourself again. And again. For example, if your answer is "I want to change him because I don't like when he does these," then ask yourself, "Why don't I like these?"

If your answer is, "Because it makes me feel embarrassed," then ask yourself why it embarrasses you. It may turn out that you do not really want to change the other person, you just want to avoid rejection or feeling not good enough in general.

Support and nurture. Part of loving someone is being supportive, encouraging them to be the best version of themselves. Sometimes, it means holding a mirror up for them to see what is, or isn't, serving them. Love cradles, nurtures and fosters growth and development. If you're having a hard time supporting or nurturing someone, ask yourself why? Peel back three layers, again. Relationships are a great way to learn about ourselves. Challenges are the perfect opportunity to find hidden fears, self-limiting beliefs, and characteristics needing some practice/work. So much of ourselves can be discovered by taking a look at the way we treat other people, especially those we love.

Chapter 6

Learn the language of Love. Love is the opposite of fear. Love is about giving, not taking. Love asks "what can I do for you?" where fear (or a lack of love) asks, "What do I get out of this?" Love can be described as receiving a gift. You cherish it, honor it, appreciate its beauty. That gift is the other person. Love honors the other person and always strives to serve, protect, nurture and build. Love speaks softly and gently. Love provides what the other needs.If you find yourself yelling, bullying, manipulating or acting aggressively towards someone you love, ask yourself how you can change this cycle of behavior When did this pattern begin? Is this something you learned growing up, or something you adapted along the way as a protective mechanism? Understanding that love means being vulnerable and open, what are some other ways you can handle the other person without making them feel badly?

Know when loving means letting go. Often times when we love someone, we have to make very difficult decisions that are for the highest good of all involved. You've heard of "tough love," and it's simply that: being tough or standing strong even when it's so difficult to do so, for the benefit of the person you love. There are situations that arise where letting go of someone is the most loving thing you can do for them. Whether it means giving them permission to leave this physical world, or leaving a relationship, it takes courage and real love to let go. Letting go of someone you love will certainly stir all sorts of emotions and fears within you. Find a way to make it easier by asking yourself what the root of this fear is. Is it attachment? If so, what meaning did you assign to this relationship that makes it so difficult to let go? What are some ways you can help yourself to heal, knowing that it's the most loving thing you can do for the other person?

Chapter 7

True love begins at home. Self-love is a requirement if you want to love someone else. You need to nurture yourself, feed your body and soul, and feel good in order to have the space to love others. If you begin to break down, you can not be anything to anyone. Loving someone else means loving yourself to good health and spirits so you can be there for them!If you treated others the way you treat yourself, would they want to be around you? How you speak to yourself is so important to overall well-being. Loving yourself means honoring yourself and acting out in all the ways you would someone else that you love. Accept yourself for all parts of you, support and nurture yourself (be your own cheerleader!), speak and act gently to yourself, and learn to let go of people, places or things that are no longer serving you!

Boost yourself up. The bigger you are, the more of you there is to go around to others you love. The more love you have within yourself, the more you have to share!

Chapter 8

Here are the keys to help you face this challenge and keep your heart open, so that you can have the abundance of love that you want and deserve.

Understand The Real Problem

The real problem is the mind. Fear lives in the mind, and the mind wants you to hang on to a situation that is known and comfortable for you. The ego-mind resists change because it is afraid of losing control and feels insecure about the unpredictability of the unknown. Love means the death of the ego, because love cannot be controlled, it can only be received and accepted. Love is fragile. One day it is there, the next day it may be gone -- like the wind. We cannot grasp the wind in our fist; we can only enjoy and appreciate it while it is there. With this awareness, be present with love, and it will grow and expand.

Practice Gratitude

A gratitude practice is of tremendous help with all matters of the heart. For example, when that relationship ends, be grateful for the good times you shared, for what this person gave you with their energy, time and heart. Thank them for being in your life, and wish them well as they move on to what's next for them. When you hold this person with love in your heart, even though they may be the one breaking up with you and even if they've already met someone else, you are healing yourself. It's love that heals your broken heart. By refusing to shut your heart down, and by facing the hurt and fear, you are able to receive all the love you need to heal and move on.

Surround Yourself With Loving Friends and Family

At a difficult time when you are, for example, going through a divorce or a difficult breakup, your youngest child has left for college or you feel betrayed by a friend, it's important to keep your heart open to receiving love and support from friends and family. Life doesn't always seem fair, but love is always there, available for us; we just have to be open to receiving it. Be careful not to expect support from people who have nothing to give or who do not wish you well. Avoid them, and focus on the people you know do love you. Sometimes a professional counselor can be just the right fit if family and friends are too overwhelmed with their own lives.

Chapter 9

Take Responsibility for How You Interpret Your Situation

Bring loving awareness to yourself, and be careful not to judge yourself or compare yourself with others. You have a choice between experiencing resentment, pain and suffering or love, peace and joy. It all depends on your interpretation of the situation. Do you perceive yourself as a victim? Or, can you accept the situation -- which doesn't mean you have to like it -- for what it is, and receive the blessing that is often revealed later on.

What if you created this very situation so that you could continue to grow and expand in love?

By taking the responsibility on your own shoulders, you are having integrity -- which portends well for you -- and you will discover a rich well of creativity, strength and wisdom inside you that you didn't know you had!

Watch the Mind

For the mind, love is a dangerous path. The mind will advise you to avoid love, but this is even more dangerous, because love is the central core of our lives. A life without love is a life that is withered and dried up.

It is because of the pain of love that millions live a
loveless life -- like a rotten seed that has never
opened to flower to it's fullest potential. If you don't
go into love, as many people have decided, then
you are stuck with your bags of potato chips! Then,
your life is a stagnant pool. You need to keep the
energy flowing, like a river that keeps on flowing to
the ocean.

Always Choose Love

Always choose love because even though there is
pain, to suffer in love is not to suffer in vain; it takes
you to higher levels of consciousness. There is a
positive, creative outcome for you. If you choose
the mind you will also suffer, but it will be useless
suffering with an unproductive outcome. Life will be
dull, and you will become neurotic from lack of love.
To be afraid of love and to be afraid of the growing
pains of love is to remain enclosed in a dark cell.

The transformation we all go through is from control
of the mind to vulnerability of the heart, and the
agony can be deep. But, you cannot have ecstasy
without going through agony. If the gold wants to be
purified, it has to pass through fire.

Love is fire.

Find your courage and love, fully and completely.
Trust and live in your heart. Love takes you from

the head to the heart and nurtures, comforts and
heals you even as you pass through the fire.

With love, the ego drops and the soul arises. Love
is food for the soul.

Conclusion

You can ask yourself, "Is this pain for my growth?" "Is my heart breaking open to give and receive even more love?" Every time your heart breaks open, yes, it's painful, but it means your heart is expanding and deepening. The pain is productive.

Learn from each experience, watch the ego and choose love. Go through the dark night and you reach a beautiful sunrise. It is only in the womb of the dark night that the sun evolves. It is only through the dark night that the morning comes.